PAPA-TUDES

PAPA-TUDES

Robert Masello

A Perigee Book

Perigee Books
are published by
The Putnam Publishing Group
200 Madison Avenue
New York, NY 10016

Published simultaneously in Canada

Library of Congress Cataloging-in-Publication Data

Masello, Robert.
Papa-tudes / Robert Masello.
p. cm.
ISBN 0-399-51742-1 (pbk.)
I. Title.
PN6162.M278 1992 91–41039 CIP
081–dc20

Cover design and illustration by Robert Korn

Printed in the United States of America
1 2 3 4 5 6 7 8 9 10

This book is printed on acid-free paper.

This book is dedicated to—who else?—my dad, whose own favorite saying was "Always wear a hat." With this timeless wisdom in my pocket, I have never wanted for direction in life.

Acknowledgments

This book could not have been written without the help of many friends, friends of friends, and family members. I am indebted to them all. The roll of honor includes the following: my wife, Laurie, my mother, Sonia, my brothers Steven and David, Mary Joan, Uncle Bobby and Aunt Jo, Robbie and Lynn, Claude and Jane Drake, David and Susan Ortega, John and Louise Catalfamo, David and Gloria Brimm, Chuck and Pam Cohen, Cathy Ward, Jennifer Castle, Bob and Diana Long, Allison Storto, Linda Ivey, Belle Lyman, Fern Brown, Nicole Plumlee, Linda Stewart, Keith Tuber, Susan Williams, Liz Stein, Charlotte Barnard, Cathee Crain, John and Jayne Spensieri, Ernestine Cookson, Mel Guenther, Erdine Ross, Melissa Peterson, Carol Weston, Robert Ackerman, Ed Abrahams, Beth Frederick, Juliet Packer, Sara Nelson, Mark and Arlene Stein, Laura Flynn and Robert S. McCarthy, Julie Schirmer, Gary Roos, Nancy Kane, Carol Spelius, Tom Cartwright, Bob Natoli, Kim Brown, Laurel

Davis, Andrew Hess, Kathy and Chris Robinson, Madeline Johnson, Chuck Filliettaz, Peter Strode, Yolanda Segovia, Marna Rough, Catherine Calvert, Janice Kaplan, Ron Dennett, Anita Cotter, Ellen Bilgore, Tom Hoster, Mark Weston, Anne Colby, Roger Friskey, et al.

A special nod must also be given to my friend and editor, Gene Brissie; without his keen editorial instincts, unswerving devotion to Truth, and the profound knowledge of human nature he acquired growing up in a series of hard-scrabble New Jersey towns, this book might not have emerged as the lasting monument that my mother assures me it is. Thank you, Gene.

PAPA-TUDES

Platitudes and Paternal Advice Worth Remembering (Most of the Time)

HOW TO USE THIS VOLUME

First, picture your father. Then, picture him with his mouth open. What is he saying? Is he reminding you, for the thousandth time, that "Money doesn't grow on trees"?

This is what we call a Papa-tude.

Or is he, perhaps, issuing a health advisory? "Cross your eyes and they'll stay that way."

This, too, is a Papa-tude.

So is "Don't count your chickens before they're hatched."

And "Keep your feet off the furniture."

And "Don't start eating until your mother sits down."

All of these are Papa-tudes—the platitudes and paternal advice that fathers, no matter how hard they might try, cannot resist saying. And that we, no matter how hard *we* might try, cannot forget.

Where do they come from? Why have they lasted so long? And what can we do about them? This book will answer none of those questions. This book is simply a compendium—though the *definitive* compendium—of everything our fathers ever said . . . over and over and over again. Some of these Papa-tudes will be heartwarmingly familiar, while others will be refreshingly new. But rest assured—every one of these things got said, and more than once, by somebody's dad. If it wasn't yours, it was somebody else's. And for that, at least, you may be grateful.

Contents

1

Dad Lays Down the Law . . .

Don't make me come upstairs.

You kids aren't going to be happy until somebody gets hurt.

You're grounded.

That's not a request; that's an order.

Pipe down in there.

One day you'll thank me for this.

Just because everyone else is doing it doesn't mean you have to.

This hurts me more than it does you.

Too much laughter turns to tears.

Go ask your mother.

You could put somebody's eye out with that.

Cut it out.

I don't care what the other kids are doing.

Enough is enough.

Not as long as you're living under my roof.

I'm only doing this for your own good.

Out of the frying pan, into the fire.

I'm at the end of my rope.

Shut up and drink your beer.

Don't you use that tone of voice with me.

Face the music.

Front and center.

Don't you dare.

Put that in your pipe and smoke it.

I wasn't born with a silver spoon in my mouth.

You've been getting away with murder.

I give you an inch, you take a mile.

Close the door—where were you born, in a barn?

Is that your lower lip, or are you drinking a plate of soup?

You're full of beans.

You made your bed, now you have to lie in it.

Don't press your luck.

You may think it's funny now.

Go play in traffic.

Children should be seen and not heard.

Don't just sit there with your teeth in your mouth.

Wipe that silly grin off your face.

Not another peep out of you.

I'm going to sell you to the gypsies.

What did I just tell you?

Bah humbug!

Children should be locked in a closet until they're old enough to read Greek.

You think I work for the electric company?

Keep your feet off the furniture.

Guilt is written all over your face.

Who died and left you king/queen?

That's the last time I'm telling you.

Button your lip.

Don't get on your high horse.

You've got champagne taste with a beer pocketbook.

Because I said so.

Do you want the back of my hand?

You're skating on thin ice.

You're getting too big for your breeches.

Well, aren't you leading the life of Riley.

Do as I say, not as I do.

Mind your p's and q's.

Is that your considered opinion?

Don't cry in public.

Can you play "Far, Far Away?"

What state are the Texas Rangers from?

Let me know if you're ever off the phone.

How many times do I have to tell you?

Why should I give you advice if you're not going to take it?

Do you think I was born yesterday?

The less you say, the better off you'll be.

All I want for Father's Day is for you kids to stop fighting.

2

Dad Cleans Us Up . . .

You only get one chance to make a good first impression.

Did you comb your hair with a beer bottle?

Never shave with a rusty razor.

Always carry a pocket comb.

No man is a hero to his valet.

Soap is just as good as shampoo.

Hang your wet towels on the bar.

Who do you think your mother is—a maid?

Cleanliness is next to godliness.

Never put anything smaller than your elbow in your ear.

If a horse gets groomed, so can you.

Never go to bed with dirty feet.

Don't pick at them—that just makes it worse.

Always wash your hands after using the bathroom.

Never cut your toenails too short—that's how they get ingrown.

Brush your teeth—once in the morning, once at night.

Put the cap back on the toothpaste.

Who threw this soap out? It's still good.

Keep the shower curtain *inside* the tub.

Never sit down on a public toilet without putting tissue down first.

A woman glows, a man perspires, a horse sweats.

Electric razors give a lousy shave.

Don't bite your fingernails.

Wash behind your ears.

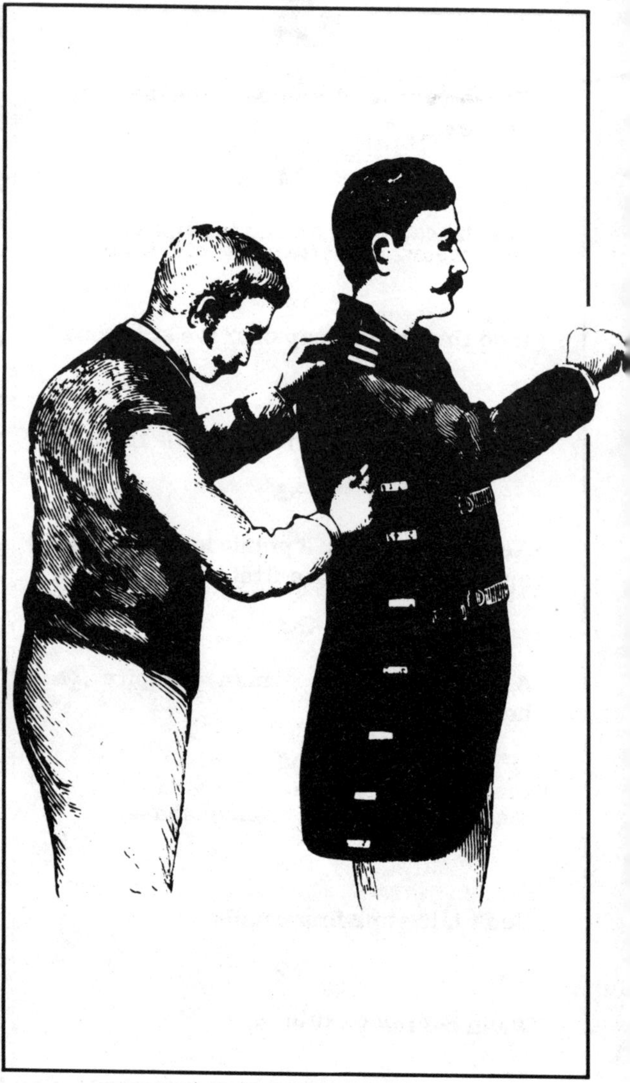

3

Dad Gets Us Dressed . . .

Never wear two patterns at one time.

You're not leaving this house dressed like that.

Always carry a handkerchief.

Your shoes should match your belt.

Nobody ever looked good in a brown suit.

Make sure your socks cover your calf.

The most important piece of apparel is a scarf.

Keep your shoes shined.

Wear your wallet in your breast pocket.

You can't go wrong in a blue blazer and gray slacks.

The bottom of your tie should touch your belt.

Clothes make the man.

Always wear clean underwear, in case you're hit by a car.

Rotate the shoes you wear—they'll last longer that way.

You look like a hobo.

Too loose is better than too tight.

If you're not sure how to dress for an occasion, overdress; you can't go wrong that way.

Keep your shoes tied, or you'll trip on the laces.

Always leave a little cuff showing.

Use a shoehorn.

4
Dad Goes to Work . . .

Don't ever make your boss look bad.

Never put off till tomorrow what you can do today.

A job worth doing is worth doing well.

Many hands make light the work.

Everytime one door closes, another one opens.

Two heads are better than one.

The cream always rises to the top.

Experience is the best teacher. Too bad she's so expensive.

Here today, gone tomorrow.

People always like to hear their own name.

Always give a firm handshake.

The harder you work, the luckier you get.

There's no free lunch.

It's all in a day's work.

Fish or cut bait.

Beggars can't be choosers.

Never look a gift horse in the mouth.

Better late than never.

Look before you leap.

The big fish eat the little fish.

Get a job.

Cross that bridge when you come to it.

I'd trust a guy in work clothes before a city slicker.

Practice doesn't make perfect—practice makes improvement.

It's a dog-eat-dog world.

Don't borrow trouble.

The early bird catches the worm.

Get all your ducks in a row.

Never hide your light under a bushel.

Don't crow before you're out of the woods.

Don't cry over spilt milk.

It's not all fun and games.

Never change horses in midstream.

Don't cut off your nose to spite your face.

The grass is always greener on the other side of the fence.

Don't put the cart before the horse.

Grin and bear it.

Don't get off on the wrong foot.

Don't give up the ship.

Make virtue of necessity.

Don't jump to conclusions.

Make hay while the sun shines.

Don't upset the applecart.

The world is your oyster.

Never buy a pig in a poke.

Never put all your eggs in one basket.

A rolling stone gathers no moss.

Stick to your guns.

Take the bull by the horns.

Don't throw the baby out with the bathwater.

Don't let the grass grow under your feet.

Be nice to the people you meet on the way up; they're the same people you might meet on the way down.

5

Dad Discusses High Finance . . .

Watch the pennies and the dollars will take care of themselves.

Rich or poor, it's nice to be rich.

The dollar is round—it rolls from pocket to pocket.

Don't count the other guy's money.

Neither a borrower nor a lender be.

Write if you get work.

Money doesn't grow on trees.

Wait till *you're* paying the bills.

I'm not made of money.

You can't draw anything out of the bank if you don't put anything in.

How'd you like to earn a nice shiny quarter?

If you're so smart, why aren't you rich?

Don't say no until you've heard the offer.

You've got to spend money to make money.

Easy come, easy go.

When I was sixteen, I was earning a living.

A penny saved is a penny earned.

A bird in the hand is worth two in the bush.

You can't cheat an honest man.

Buy low, sell high.

What's the bottom line?

A fool and his money are soon parted.

Don't be penny-wise and pound-foolish.

Half a loaf is better than none.

Never give a sucker an even break.

Shirtsleeves to shirtsleeves, in three generations.

Crime doesn't pay.

If you steal, make it a million dollars so you can buy your way out.

Don't take any wooden nickels.

Set what you think is a fair price for your work—then ask for double.

If a deal sounds too good to be true, it probably is.

Another day, another dollar.

Only gamble what you can afford to lose.

Save up all your pennies and be cunning as a fox, and you'll always have some money in the old tobacco box.

Never mix business with pleasure.

It's not what you earn but what you save that keeps you out of the poor house.

A dollar weighs heavy in your pocket when you see someone hungry.

The good things in life are free.

Don't ever be afraid to buy the best.

You get what you pay for.

In for a dime, in for a dollar.

When a man says it's not the money but the principle of the thing, you can be darn sure it's the money.

6
Dad on Dining . . .

Chew before you swallow.

If you can afford to eat out, you can afford to leave a good tip.

Don't talk with your mouth full.

Don't fill up on bread.

How do you know you don't like it if you've never even tried it?

Children are starving in China.

Carrots are good for your eyes.

Fish is brain food.

Go Dutch.

Don't play with your food.

Breakfast is the most important meal of the day.

Your eyes are bigger than your stomach.

If you're overheated, don't drink cold liquids too fast; you can give yourself a heart attack that way.

Eat where the truck drivers eat.

Have some more steak—steak can't hurt you.

Know which side your bread is buttered on.

You can tell a restaurant's good if there are lots of cars in the parking lot.

Never eat at a place with a view—they're selling the view, not the food.

Finish what's on your plate before you ask for more.

Don't wash your food down.

Always order your liquor by the brand name.

If you're somebody's guest, order from the middle of the menu.

Hunger is the best sauce.

Never order your liquor by the brand name; they give you the cheap stuff anyway.

No one should see laws or sausages being made.

If you want something sweet, eat a piece of fruit.

Don't spoil your appetite.

Keep your elbows off the table.

If you're going to order it, you'd better eat it.

7

Dad Gets Practical . . .

You don't have to like everybody, but everybody can like you.

Cross your eyes and they'll stay that way.

Never write down anything you wouldn't want to hear read aloud in court.

Always buy American.

Fill out the warranty.

Get it in writing.

If you see a good two-by-four, buy it.

If you can't run with the big dogs, don't jump off the porch.

There's always Nebraska State Teachers' College.

Sow your wild oats.

Nobody likes a know-it-all.

Loose lips sink ships.

If you're good at something, you don't need to tell anybody; they'll find out for themselves.

Use your noodle.

Don't be a nosy Parker.

It's all grist for the mill.

Old shoes are the most comfortable.

Dogs can smell fear.

Never walk under a ladder.

He travels fastest who travels alone.

Never hide under a pile of leaves—a car could run over them.

Never let the flag touch the ground.

Too many cooks spoil the broth.

What does *Consumer Reports* say?

Always take the time to write.

You can't see the forest for the trees.

Curiosity killed the cat.

You can't have your cake and eat it too.

First things first.

You can't throw dirt without getting some on yourself.

Two can play that game.

Give the devil his due.

Women and children first.

Let the chips fall where they may.

Show me your company and I'll show you what you are.

You live and learn.

Don't make a mountain out of a molehill.

Always carry jumper cables in your trunk.

You're only as good as your tools.

Don't sit too close to the television; you'll ruin your eyes.

Don't start anything you don't plan to finish.

The only way out is through.

Don't jump if you can't see the bottom.

Only smart people worry about doing a good job.

When you've got a big project to do, go at it piecemeal.

Remember—the teachers are just as nervous as you are.

Never drink when you're feeling sorry for yourself.

If I act like that when I get old, shoot me.

House guests are like fish—after three days, they both stink.

Don't ever be ashamed to ask a question.

That's what you've got feet for.

You can catch more flies with honey than vinegar.

You can choose your friends, but you can't choose your family.

No matter how you slice it, it's still baloney.

Drive as if everybody else on the road is an idiot.

The squeaky wheel gets the grease.

There's safety in numbers.

Haste makes waste.

Crack your knuckles and you'll get arthritis.

Count to ten before you speak.

There's no use getting into a pissing contest with a skunk.

Don't go off half-cocked.

Be polite to Aunt May.

Don't rock the boat.

Look it up in the dictionary.

Don't bite off more than you can chew.

That and a token will get you a ride on the subway.

You have to cut your clothes according to your cloth.

There's no time like the present.

Keep your powder dry.

8
Dad Plays Ball . . .

Never argue with the ump.

It's not whether you win or lose, it's how you play the game.

Never back down from a fight.

Keep your eye on the ball.

Always play by the rules.

Never swing at the first pitch.

Hold the ball by the laces.

Don't be a tattletale.

A good offense is the best defense.

When the going gets tough, the tough get going.

Never hit below the belt.

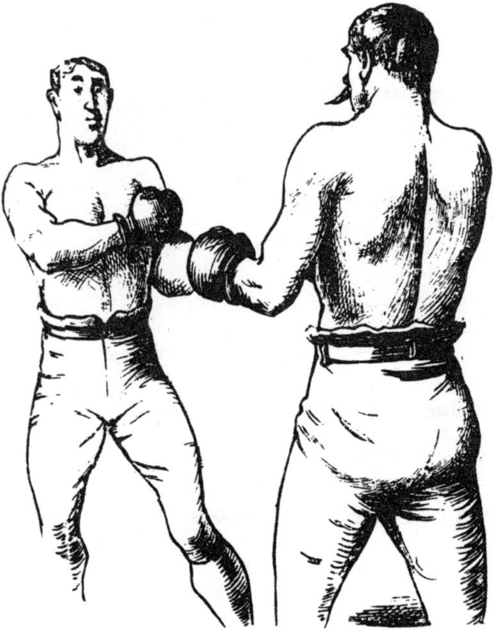

You win some, you lose some, and some are rained out . . . but you suit up for every ballgame.

The race is to the swift.

Nice guys finish last.

Boys will be boys.

Buckle down.

Get a move on.

Get on the stick.

Get the lead out.

Sink or swim.

Tie goes to the runner.

It ain't over till it's over.

Stroke the ball; don't try to kill it.

There's nothing wrong with playing right field.

Nobody likes a sore loser.

Winning isn't everything.

There's only one captain.

If you can't play fair, it's not fair to play.

Just do your best.

All work and no play makes Jack a dull boy.

Slow and steady wins the race.

It's easy to be a Monday-morning quarterback.

You can't change the rules in the middle of the game.

Put up your dukes.

Let me feel your muscles.

There's no *i* in team.

9

Dad Goes on Vacation . . .

Don't make me pull over.

Can't any of you fold up the map the way it was?

If you have to go, go now.

We're not lost; I know where I'm going.

Buckle up.

That better not melt in the car.

Who's got the Wash n' Dries?

If you don't keep it down back there, you're going to get out and walk.

Put that back in the glove department.

Let's play geography.

We're almost there.

Look at the cows!

Do any of you have any idea what gas costs?

Look at the horsies!

It says Vacancy—that's good enough for me.

Nobody goes anywhere until we unpack this car.

We'll take one room—with five cots.

A fan's just as good as an air conditioner.

They *expect* you to take the towels—it's already figured into the room bill.

I need a vacation from my vacation.

Keep your shoes on, or you're liable to step on a piece of glass.

Say cheese!

Flying's too expensive.

There are two classes of travel—first-class, and with children.

Keep it up, and next summer there won't *be* any vacation.

10
Dad Waxes Romantic . . .

It's as easy to fall in love with a rich girl as a poor one.

There's always another streetcar coming around the corner.

Leave the dance with the girl that brung you.

The man who marries for money earns it.

Beauty's only skin deep.

There's plenty of fish in the sea.

Don't get married until you plan to have babies.

I never knew what happiness was until I got married—and then it was too late.

Never go to bed angry.

Why buy the cow when you can get the milk for free?

Marry in haste; repent at leisure.

Opposites attract.

Familiarity breeds contempt.

Variety is the spice of life.

Absence makes the heart grow fonder.

If you want to break up with a girl, make her think it's her fault.

All's fair in love and war.

A woman is only a woman, but a good cigar is a smoke.

The course of true love never did run smooth.

Love makes the world go round.

It's better to have loved and lost than never to have loved at all.

In spring, a young man's fancy turns to thoughts of love.

Hell hath no fury like a woman scorned.

You'll get over it.

If she'll do it for you, she'll do it for anyone.

Don't do anything you'll be ashamed to tell me in the morning.

Be home by eleven.

Call.

Handsome is as handsome does.

Never hit a woman.

Money, sex, and religion—those are the big three you've got to agree on.

Eat plenty of oysters.

Never stifle a tender impulse.

Love flies out the window if there's no money coming in the door.

Want to know what she'll look like in twenty years, look at her mother.

11
Dad Grows Philosophical . . .

The apple doesn't fall far from the tree.

Laugh and the world laughs with you, cry and you cry alone.

A friend in need is a friend indeed.

If everyone else was jumping off the Brooklyn Bridge, would you do it?

Necessity is the mother of invention.

From your lips to God's ear.

If you want to make an omelette, you've got to break some eggs.

Lie down with dogs, you get up with fleas.

A little knowledge is a dangerous thing.

Just because you're paranoid, that doesn't mean you're not being followed.

Never play cards with a guy named Doc, never eat at a place called Mom's, and never go to bed with anybody who's got more troubles than you have.

It's better to light a candle than curse the darkness.

Fools rush in where angels fear to tread.

What goes around comes around.

It's no use bolting the barn door after the horse is gone.

Strike while the iron's hot.

Be careful what you wish for; you're liable to get it.

Every tub sits on its own bottom.

Don't pat yourself on the back so hard you break your elbow.

You won't believe it now, but someday you'll look back on this and laugh.

It's better than a sharp stick in the eye.

Never draw to an inside straight.

Everything in moderation.

He who laughs last, laughs best.

He puts his pants on one leg at a time, too.

If you can't stand the heat, get out of the kitchen.

Brevity is the soul of wit.

Birds of a feather flock together.

Blood is thicker than water.

It's an ill wind that blows nobody any good.

Let bygones be bygones.

Knock on wood.

You can lead a horse to water, but you can't make him drink.

So who said life is fair?

We get too soon old, and too late smart.

Still waters run deep.

Empty heads make the most noise.

You can't judge a book by its cover.

Everything comes out in the wash.

If the shoe fits, wear it.

You'll always find your keys in the last place you look.

Seeing is believing.

There's many a slip twixt the cup and the lip.

I'm from Missouri—show me.

Mighty oaks from little acorns grow.

Every dog has his day.

Every cloud has a silver lining.

He who lives by the sword, dies by the sword.

Laughter is the best medicine.

Discretion is the better part of valor.

Ignorance is bliss.

Success has a thousand parents, but failure is always an orphan.

Everybody wants to go to heaven, but nobody wants to die.

Even a broken clock is right twice a day.

Never let the camel get its nose in the tent.

It always rains after a long dry spell.

Stop and smell the roses.

Actions speak louder than words.

The die is cast.

Two wrongs don't make a right.

Never hit a man when he's down.

Have the courage of your convictions.

Don't worry—he'll get mad in the same pants he got glad in.

Common sense is harder to come by than a college education.

An ordinary working stiff has more real friends than a bank president.

Always go out the same door you came in.

Sugar catches flies . . . but who wants them?

If you swallowed the camel, why strain at a gnat?

Apples will grow again.

Make like a duck—stay calm on the surface, but paddle like hell underneath.

Youth is wasted on the young.

The more people I meet, the more I like my dog.

If everyone agreed, it wouldn't be a horse race.